in your NEIGHBOURHOOD

British
Mammals

Clare Collinson

W

FRANKLIN WATTS
LONDON • SYDNEY

Franklin Watts
First published in Great Britain in paperback in 2018 by The Watts
Publishing Group.

Copyright © The Watts Publishing Group 2016

All rights reserved.

Planning and production by Discovery Books Limited
Managing Editor: Laura Durman
Editor: Clare Collinson
Design: sprout.uk.com
Picture research: Clare Collinson

ISBN: 978 1 4451 3639 4

Printed in China

Franklin Watts
An imprint of
Hachette Children's Group
Part of The Watts Publishing Group
Carmelite House
50 Victoria Embankment
London EC4Y 0DZ

An Hachette UK Company
www.hachette.co.uk
www.franklinwatts.co.uk

FSC
www.fsc.org
MIX
Paper from
responsible sources
FSC® C104740

Picture credits: Alamy: p. 12 (David Boag), p. 20t
(Paul Lindley), p. 23t (Michael Clark/FLPA/Imagebroker), p. 29b
(Chris Brignell); Bigstock: title page (PaulMaguire), p. 4b (krisrobin),
p. 7 (both) (CreativeNaturePhotography), p. 8l (Steve Meese),
p. 8r (stefanholm), p. 10 (kwasny221), p. 11b (Elina), p. 13t (koi88),
p. 14b (PaulMaguire), p. 15t (Nosnibor137), p. 15b (Tom Linster),
p. 25b (bikeworldtravel), p. 26t (Bardofthebroch), p. 27t (kogb);
FLPA: p. 6t (Gerard Lacz), p. 9t (Andrew Mason), p. 11t (Ingo
Arndt), p. 14t (Derek Middleton), p. 16 (John Hawkins), p. 19bl
(Paul Sawer), p. 22 (David Hosking), p. 25c (Michael Krabs/
Imagebroker), p. 30b (Michael Durham); Shutterstock: pp. 3, 31
(Eric Isselee, Marina Jay, Kirsanov Valeriy Vladimirovich), p. 4t
(Piotr Krzeslak), p. 5 (Richard Bowden), pp. 6b, 19br (Erni),
pp. 9b, 13b (Bildagentur Zoonar GmbH), p. 17 (Steve
Oehlenschlager), p. 18 (Kdamian), pp. 19tr, 21t (Stephan Morris),
p. 20b (Mark Caunt), p. 21b (S. Cooper Digital), p. 23b (Jerome
Whittingham), p. 24 (Matt Gibson), p. 25tr (MilanB), p. 26b
(majusko95), p. 27b (Gerald Marella), p. 28b (Guido Bissattini),
p. 28t (Piotr Kamionka), p. 29t (Gail Johnson), p. 30t (a40757), p. 31
(cmnaumann, Robert Eastman, Iakov Filimonov, Adam Gryko, S-F).

Cover photo: Bigstock (Kyslynskyy).

Every attempt has been made to clear copyright. Should there be any
inadvertent omission please apply to the publisher for rectification.

Useful websites

Bat Conservation Trust
www.bats.org.uk
Find out about British bat species, as well as what is
being done to help bats and protect their habitats.

British Hedgehog Preservation Society
www.britishhedgehogs.org.uk
Information about hedgehogs, including how to
encourage them into your neighbourhood.

Hare Preservation Trust
www.hare-preservation-trust.co.uk
Information about brown hares, including the reasons
for their decline and what can be done to help them.

The Mammal Society
www.mammal.org.uk
Find out about British mammals, their conservation
and what you can do to help them.

The Wildlife Trusts UK
www.wildlifetrusts.org
Find a nature reserve near you. There is a species
explorer page with information about British mammals.

Woodland Trust: Mammals
*www.woodlandtrust.org.uk/visiting-woods/trees-woods-
and-wildlife/animals/mammals/*
Information about woodland mammals.

Wildlife Watch
www.wildlifewatch.org.uk
Find out how to take part in a 'wildlife watch' and
other environmental activities in your local area.

*Note to parents and teachers: Every effort has been
made to ensure that these websites contain no
inappropriate or offensive material. However, because
of the nature of the Internet, it is impossible to guarantee
that the contents of these sites will not be altered. We
strongly advise that Internet access is supervised by a
responsible adult.*

Contents

Words that appear in **bold** in the text are explained in the glossary.

Your neighbourhood

What kind of neighbourhood do you live in? Is your home in the town or the countryside? It might be halfway up a mountain, or by the sea. Wherever you live, you will be amazed at how much mammal life there is right on your doorstep.

Urban habitats

Even in the busiest cities, there will be small **rodents**, such as grey squirrels, and larger **predators**, such as foxes. Urban parks provide an ideal **habitat** for mammals of all shapes and sizes, right up to **grazers**, such as deer.

In the countryside

The British countryside is teeming with mammal life, from the tiny pygmy shrew to the wild ponies and even wild boar that roam our **moors** and forests.

What is a mammal?

The group of animals known as mammals includes about 5,000 species worldwide, including humans. All mammals have certain things in common. They all:
• breathe air
• have a backbone
• are **warm-blooded**
• have hair or fur on their bodies, at least for some of their lives
• feed their young with milk, produced in the mother's body.

The pygmy shrew is one of Britain's smallest mammals.

Grey squirrels can often be seen in city parks and gardens.

Half of all the grey seals in the world are found around the coast of Britain.

By the sea

If you live by the coast, or visit the seaside for your holidays, you might see some British sea mammals, such as seals. If you are lucky, you may even spot a leaping dolphin or the fin of a minke whale.

Britain's mammals

There are around 100 species of wild mammal living in Britain and around its coasts. Some are known as 'native'. This means they were here when Britain split from mainland Europe and became an island around 8,000 years ago. Others are 'introduced', which means they were either brought here deliberately by people or they arrived accidentally, for example on ships.

Mice and rats

You may not even have to leave home to find the little mammals on this page. Mice might be living right under your feet, and rats may be very close by.

House mice
House mice make their homes beneath floorboards and in the gaps between walls. They feed on any crumbs and scraps left lying around. They even raid our cupboards.

Telltale signs and sounds
Mouse droppings look like tiny black seeds, and are a sure sign that these little pests are about. You might also hear them scuffling around, especially after dark.

Rat about!
Brown rats eat whatever food they can find, from fruit and seeds to human food waste.

House mice come out at night to look for food.

Dirty dwellings

You may think that rats are dirty animals but, in fact, they keep themselves very clean. It's just that they often live in dirty places, and can carry diseases.

*Brown rats (left) are often found **scavenging** near rubbish, around damp drains and in sewers.*

Big teeth

Mice and rats belong to a group of animals called rodents. The **order** of rodents makes up more than 40 per cent of all known species of mammal. All rodents have two sharp **incisor** teeth in their upper and lower jaw, which grow all the time. Rodents have to gnaw things to stop their teeth growing too long.

Smallest rodent

Harvest mice are the smallest of all European rodents. They often weigh as little as 4 g.

Country mouse

The wood mouse is one of the most common small mammals in Britain. Wood mice live in underground **burrows** in woodlands and fields.

Wood mice (right) feed on berries and seeds.

Harvest mice (above) live in fields of cereal crops, such as wheat and oats.

Squirrels, voles and dormice

Squirrels are among our most familiar mammals. You'll find them wherever there are trees. Voles and dormice live mostly in the countryside, and you may find them harder to spot!

Nut nibbler

This bushy-tailed visitor to the bird feeder is a grey squirrel. You will see grey squirrels in woodlands and parks, and they often visit gardens that have a plentiful supply of nuts.

Food stores

Look out for grey squirrels making food stores in the autumn. They often bury acorns and beech nuts at the base of trees. They return to dig them up in winter, when food is scarce.

Nibbled cones

If you find the nibbled remains of cones at the base of a tree, you will know a red squirrel is about. You can find them in **coniferous** woodland in the north of England and in Scotland.

Grey squirrels are expert climbers.

With its distinctive red fur, our native squirrel is easy to recognise.

Non-native newcomer

The grey squirrel was first introduced from North America in the 19th century. Today, it is more common in Britain than our native red squirrel.

The secret life of voles

Field voles are very common, but you will be lucky to find one! They spend their time in long grass, hiding from predators. As you walk along a river, you might hear a water vole as it plops into the water from its secret underground burrow.

Vole stats

- **There are 75 million field voles in Britain, making them the most common of all British mammals.**
- **The water vole is the most rapidly declining mammal in Britain. Since the 1970s, their numbers have fallen by more than 90 per cent to around 220,000.**

You might see a water vole on the bank of a slow-moving river.

You can recognise a dormouse by its golden-brown fur, bushy tail and big, black eyes.

Sleepy rodent

Dormice spend almost all their lives in trees and more than half the year asleep! They **hibernate** from October to April and go to sleep whenever it is cold or food is hard to find.

Rodent relatives

Like rats and mice, squirrels, voles and dormice are rodents. In spite of their name, dormice are not true mice, but belong to a separate family of their own.

Hedgehogs

Everyone knows the prickly hedgehog, with its body covered in spines and its long snout. Hedgehogs live in all parts of Britain, so you are sure to have them snuffling around your neighbourhood.

Hog habitats

As you might guess from their name, hedgehogs like to live in hedgerows. You can also find them in woodlands, parks and gardens.

A gardener's friend

Hedgehogs are popular with gardeners, as they love to eat snails and slugs, which often damage garden plants. Hedgehogs are not fussy eaters. Their diet also includes worms, caterpillars, earwigs, baby rodents, frogs and birds' eggs.

Night feeders

During the day, hedgehogs sleep in nests made of grass, among leaves or in hollow logs. They come out when it gets dark, and can travel 1–2 km each night in search of food.

Spiny species

An adult hedgehog's body is covered in up to 7,000 sharp spines. Hedgehogs are the only spiny mammals in Britain.

A winter rest

This hedgehog is hibernating. It will not wake up until spring. If you come across a hibernating hedgehog, don't wake it up.

Hedgehogs in danger

It is thought that the number of hedgehogs in Britain has dropped by around 50 per cent in the last 25 years to around one million today. One reason for this may be the loss of hedgehog habitats, such as hedgerows. Also, many thousands are killed each year on Britain's roads.

Helping hogs

If you have a garden, one of the best ways to help hedgehogs is to leave out some food for them in the evening. You can give them unsweetened muesli in a shallow bowl, or meat-based pet food (nothing fishy). Leave some fresh water, too, but don't leave out milk, because this can make them ill.

Hegdehog-friendly gardens

Hedgehogs don't like tidy gardens. Piles of leaves and logs are good places for them to nest. Many gardens have high fences, so it helps if there are small gaps at the bottom to allow hedgehogs to get in and out. You can find out more about hedgehog-friendly gardens on the website of the British Hedgehog Preservation Society.

Shrews and moles

Shrews and moles are common throughout Britain, but they are very hard to spot. Shrews spend their time in burrows and scurrying about in the undergrowth. Moles live almost all their lives underground, but they leave telltale signs for us to see.

Shy shrews

There are almost 42 million shrews in Britain, but they like to stay hidden. You may hear their high-pitched squeaking sounds near hedgerows and long grass.

Frequent feeders

Shrews eat two to three times their own body weight in insects, slugs, snails and worms every day. They must eat every two or three hours, just to stay alive.

Tiny mammal

The pygmy shrew weighs only 2.4–6.1 g and its body measures just 4–6 cm. Only the pipistrelle bat (see page 22) is as small.

You can recognise a shrew by its tiny eyes, small ears and long, pointy nose.

Mole mounds

If you come across little mounds of fresh soil heaped up in a field or garden lawn (right), you can be sure that a mole is tunnelling below ground. With a population of over 30 million in Britain, there are lots of moles about!

Soil shifters

Moles are small mammals with spade-like front legs, which they use for burrowing underground. They can dig 20 m of tunnels in one day, shifting 540 times their own body weight in soil! The molehills we see are the soil they push to the surface.

Finding food

Moles are almost blind and use their sensitive noses to find their food. They eat over half their own body weight in worms and insect grubs every day.

Mole watching

If you see a molehill, sit quietly nearby. If you are very lucky, you will see a flurry of earth and the mole will pop up to sniff the air.

Close relatives

Shrews and moles belong to the same order of mammals, called Soricomorpha (meaning 'shrew-shaped').

Moles hardly ever come up from their tunnels, but occasionally they emerge above ground.

Rabbits and hares

If you live in the countryside, you have probably seen wild rabbits and hares, with their long ears and fluffy tails. Look out for them in the early morning or evening, when they hop around fields and hillsides, nibbling on grass and plants.

The burrowers

Look at the rabbits below sitting outside their burrow. Rabbits live in systems of connecting underground tunnels called warrens. Their warrens can house up to 100 rabbits.

Rabbit clues

You can sometimes see the entrances to rabbit warrens on grassy banks, in hedgerows and at the edge of fields. The holes are usually about 15–20 cm across. If there is loose soil around the hole, you will know there are rabbits inside. You might also see small piles of rabbit droppings nearby.

Rabbits are most active at night, but sometimes come out of their warrens during the day.

Staying safe

Rabbits have lots of enemies, including foxes and birds of prey. If they sense danger, they thump the ground with their back legs to warn others. When they are being chased, they run in a zigzag motion to confuse the predator.

Rabbits produce lots of round droppings. They are brown or green and about 10 mm across.

Boxing match

Brown hares are usually shy creatures, but during the **breeding season** in spring, you may see them chasing each other in broad daylight. You might also see a 'boxing match' like this one, with a female standing on her back legs, fighting a male.

Built for speed

Hares are the fastest land mammal in Britain. They can reach speeds of up to 72 kph – that means they can run 100 m in 5 seconds!

Spot the difference

Thought you saw a rabbit ... or was it a hare? A good way to tell the difference is to look at the animal's ears. A hare's ears are longer than those of a rabbit and they have black tips.

Rare hares

The number of brown hares in Britain has fallen by about 80 per cent in the last hundred years, from around 4 million to about 800,000. You can find out about the reasons for this and what is being done to help hares on the website of the Hare Preservation Trust.

Clever camouflage

If you live in the north of England, or in Scotland, you might catch sight of a mountain hare. They are easier to see in the summer, when their coats are brown. In winter, when it is snowy, their coats turn white.

In winter, a mountain hare's white coat helps to keep it hidden from predators.

Foxes

No matter where you live in Britain, you are likely to have foxes in your neighbourhood. Of all British mammals, these dog-like creatures are among the best survivors.

Fox habitats

Foxes have **adapted** well to modern British life, and many have set up home in our cities, towns and suburbs. They also live in a range of other habitats, from farmland to mountains.

City living

What is this fox doing by the rubbish bin? Foxes are natural scavengers, with a keen sense of smell. They are also skilful hunters and will eat just about anything they can find, from crabs, birds and rodents to beetles, worms and fruit.

In the family

Foxes belong to the order of mammals called carnivores (flesh eaters). Within that order, they belong to a family called canidae, which includes wolves and pet dogs.

In our towns and cities, foxes find much of their food in dustbins and rubbish tips.

*Fox **cubs** are unable to see or hear when they are born, but by the time they are four weeks old they begin to come into the open.*

Fox homes

Foxes live in family groups in underground dens called earths. They sometimes dig the earths themselves, but they also use holes made by other animals such as badgers.

Barks and calls

You might see a fox from your window when it comes out to feed at night. But you are more likely to hear one. Foxes make a range of barking sounds and calls that might wake you in the middle of the night!

Scent signs

If a fox has moved in to your neighbourhood you might detect its smell. Foxes use their sharp, tangy scent to mark their **territory**.

Safe distance

Foxes may look cute and cuddly, but they can sometimes be aggressive. If you see one, it's best not to get too close.

Badgers, weasels and stoats

Many of us have a soft spot for badgers, with their striking, black-and-white faces and playful behaviour. Stoats and weasels look quite different from badgers, but they are in the same family of mammals.

Badger habitats

Badgers usually make their homes in woodland, near hedgerows and in fields. They sometimes come into people's gardens at night to look for food, such as slugs, worms and small mammals.

Family homes

Badgers live in family groups, in underground burrows called setts. A sett is a complex maze of connecting chambers and tunnels, with as many as 40 entrances.

Sett spotting

If you find a hole in the ground, in a wood or hedgerow, it may be the entrance to a badger sett. Check the size and shape of the hole. It should be 25–30 cm wide, and be shaped like a capital D.

Smallest carnivore

The weasel is the smallest carnivore in Britain, with a body measuring just 17–25 cm. You can recognise it by the orangey-brown fur on its back, and its white belly and throat. Weasels feed mainly on small mammals, such as voles and mice, but they will also steal eggs from birds' nests.

Stoats and their coats

Stoats look very similar to weasels. The easiest way to tell them apart is to look at their tails. A stoat's tail is longer, and it has a black tip. In some parts of Britain, a stoat's coat turns white in winter.

When hunting, weasels (above) often sniff their surroundings before darting down into burrows or tunnels to chase their prey.

Even when a stoat gets its white winter coat, the tip of its tail stays black.

You can tell this is a stoat by the black tip of its tail.

Polecats and pine martens

Polecats and pine martens used to be common in Britain but they were known for killing chickens, so many were killed as pests. By the early 20th century, both species were rare. Now protected by law, they have recently been making a comeback.

Pine martens

Pine martens are very rare in England and Wales, but there are around 3,500 living in Scotland. They are excellent climbers and usually live in forests. They also visit gardens, and have even set up home in people's lofts.

Polecats

You may have polecats in your neighbourhood if you live in the countryside in Wales or central England. You can recognise one by the white markings on its ears and face.

Fierce hunters

Polecats and pine martens are beautiful creatures, but they are fierce hunters. They have sharp **canines**, which they use to kill rabbits and other prey with a deadly bite to the neck.

You might spot polecats in woods and hedgerows.

All in the family

- Polecats and pine martens are members of the weasel family.
- Polecats look very similar to ferrets, their **domesticated** relatives.

You will know a pine marten (below) by the creamy-yellow patch on its throat and neck.

Otters and mink

Otters and mink make their homes on riverbanks, by lakes and on the coast. American mink are much smaller than otters, but from a distance it's easy to mistake one for the other.

Introduced predator

First introduced from the United States in 1929, American mink are not native to Britain. They escaped from fur farms and are now commonly found in the wild.

Otter spotting

Otters are lively, intelligent mammals. The best time to see them is at dawn, and the trick is to be very patient!

A welcome return

Otters had almost disappeared from English waterways by the 1970s. Fortunately, thanks to **conservation** efforts and cleaner rivers, today they can once again be found throughout Britain.

Otters are a delight to watch as they slide about on riverbanks.

American mink are fierce predators of fish, water voles and water birds.

Otter or mink?

A good way to tell otters from American mink is to look at their fur. Otters have light brown fur, while American mink have much darker fur, which sometimes looks black when wet.

Bats

If you go outside on a warm evening, look out for bats, swooping, circling, and twisting above your head. Bats can be found all over Britain, living in cities and towns as well as in the countryside.

Seasonal menu

The best time to see bats is on a fine evening between April and August, when there are lots of flying insects about. All British bats feed on insects, such as moths, flies and midges.

Flying mammals

Bats are the only mammals that can fly. Their wings are not made of feathers, but are like hands, with skin stretched over long finger bones.

Small bat, big appetite

Like all bats, the tiny pipistrelle bat has a huge appetite. It comes out to feed at dusk and can gobble up 3,000 insects in one night. Of the 18 species of bat living in Britain, the pipistrelle is the smallest. It weighs 3–7 g and its body is 35–45 mm long.

The pipistrelle bat is the most common British bat.

*This brown long-eared bat is **roosting** in someone's loft.*

Time to rest
Most bats spend each day resting, and in winter they hibernate. They sleep upside-down in old buildings, barns, caves and holes in trees. Bats do not like to be disturbed, so if you see a roosting or hibernating bat, do not go near it.

Telltale signs
Bat droppings look like tiny black seeds, a bit like mouse droppings. But they are softer than mouse droppings and will crumble to dust if you pick them up with a tissue.

Helping bats
The number of bats declined greatly in the 20th century and some species of bat are now very rare. All bats are protected by law in Britain. You can help them by putting up a **bat box**. You can find out more about how to do this on the website of the Bat Conservation Trust.

Bat stats
- Bats make up the second largest order of mammals after rodents.
- Nearly one quarter of the world's mammal species are bats.

Bat boxes provide bats with safe places to roost.

Deer

If you walk quietly through a large wood in the early morning you will probably catch sight of a deer. It is thought there are more deer in Britain today than at any other time in the last 1,000 years.

Deer habitats

Deer live in a wide variety of habitats throughout Britain, from parks, forests and woodlands, to mountains and moors. Sometimes they even find their way into urban gardens in search of food.

Deer parks

The easiest way to see deer is to visit one of Britain's deer parks. Here, you will find large herds of deer, which are quite used to the sight and sound of humans nearby.

Largest land mammal

The magnificent mammal below is a male red deer. Growing to around 1.3 m at the shoulder, red deer are the largest of all wild land mammals in Britain. The males have impressive, branching antlers, which can grow to 1 m across.

Roe deer

Roe deer are the most common of all British deer. They live on their own or in small family groups, feeding on a wide variety of plants and young trees.

Fallow deer

Fallow deer were introduced to Britain by the Normans almost 1,000 years ago. They are the most common deer to be kept in parks, but you will also find them in woodland.

Watching deer

The best time of day to see deer in the wild is in the early morning or in the evening when they are grazing or browsing for food. Look out for their distinctive tracks in soft ground.

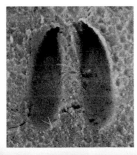

Deer walk on two-hoofed toes, making prints with two holes called 'slots'.

*Roe deer live on their own or in small family groups. You will know one by its distinctive white **rump**.*

Native and introduced

There are six species of deer in Britain, but only the red deer and roe deer are native. Fallow deer, Chinese water deer, muntjac and sika deer are all non-native species.

In summer, you can recognise fallow deer by the white spots on their backs.

Seals, whales and dolphins

You might think you are unlikely to see seals, whales and dolphins in Britain, but there are plenty of these exciting marine mammals living around our coast.

Spotting seals

Britain is home to two species of seal, the grey seal and the common seal. A good time to spot them is during the breeding season. Grey seals breed in the autumn, while common seals breed in the summer.

Seals on the shore

Seals sometimes come to land to rest, but it's easiest to see them when they come ashore to give birth to their young, or pups. Common seal pups can swim very soon after they are born. Grey seal pups remain on land for about two or three weeks before entering the water.

Seals in the sea

Seals are excellent swimmers and can spend up to 30 minutes underwater at a time. When you're by the coast, keep your eyes on the water. You might see one, like this common seal, bobbing its head above the water.

Grey seals pups (above) are usually born in October or November. You can recognise one by its long, straight nose.

This common seal has come up to the surface to breathe air.

Minke whales often swim in shallow waters near to the British coast.

Whale watching

You might expect to find whales only in deep oceans, but they are a surprisingly common sight close to the British coast. Look out for them from a high-up place on the shore. If you are lucky, you will glimpse one as it comes to the surface.

Sea sifter

The whale you are most likely to see is the minke whale (pronounced minkee). Instead of teeth, minke whales have special plates called baleen. They use these comb-like plates to sift small fish and other food from the water.

Marine acrobats

Dolphins, such as the bottlenose dolphins below, are highly intelligent and sociable creatures, and among the most friendly wild mammals towards humans. If you catch sight of one, look out for the blowhole on the top of its head. When a dolphin comes to the surface, it uses its blowhole to breathe.

Dolphins are fast swimmers, and love to dive in and out of the water.

Survival experts

You are probably familiar with many British mammals, but you might be surprised by some of the ancient native species that can be seen in Britain today.

The beaver is back

Once hunted for its fur, the beaver was **extinct** in Britain by the 16th century. In 2009, conservationists released a small number of these large rodents into the wild in Scotland. Since then, beavers have also been released in Wales and southwest England.

The return of the wild boar

Until recently, there had been no wild boar roaming free in Britain for hundreds of years. In the late 20th century, some captive boar escaped from farms and began to breed in the wild. Now, hundreds of these bristly beasts can be found living freely in our forests and woodlands.

Wild boar will eat almost anything they can find, from roots, leaves and fruit to small mammals and birds' eggs.

After a break of hundreds of years, wild beavers are once again building dams in Britain.

Wild engineers

Beavers are known for their ability to construct dams across rivers, using sticks, logs and stones. The dams raise the level of the water around the beavers' dens (called lodges). This helps to protect the lodges from predators.

Welsh mountain ponies (above) can still be seen roaming wild in the hills and valleys of Wales.

Running free

Wild ponies have roamed our land for over 100,000 years, and you can still see small numbers of truly wild ponies in some parts of Britain. You can also find semi-wild or feral ponies in forests, and on moors and mountainsides. These ponies often have owners, but they are free to roam wherever they want.

Fierce feline

This beautiful cat (right) may look a bit like a domestic tabby, but you wouldn't want to give this one a cuddle! It is one of around 400 wildcats living in Scotland. Wildcats haven't been seen in the wild in England or Wales since the 19th century.

You can tell this is a wildcat from the distinctive black stripes on its tail.

Watching mammals

Wherever you live in Britain, you won't have to go far to find mammals in your neighbourhood. Many mammals stay hidden, but once you start looking you'll be amazed how many signs and tracks they leave behind.

Be prepared
When you look for wildlife, it's a good idea to take a notebook and pen, so you can keep a record of anything you find. Binoculars and a camera are useful, too.

Dropping clues
The size and shape of droppings will help you know which mammal left them behind.

Mammal homes
Look for mammals' burrows near to hedgerows and trees.

Tracks and prints
You may find mammal tracks in the snow, or soft ground. Each mammal has its own distinctive tracks and prints.

Other clues
Look out for the nibbled remains of nuts and cones left by squirrels. If you find scratch marks on trees, you may be near a badger sett. Badgers like to sharpen their claws on trees or logs.

These are the droppings of a deer.

Spotting tip

Mammals are always on the lookout for danger, and will disappear quickly if they detect you. You will have a better chance of seeing them if you walk slowly and quietly.

These tracks were made by a badger.

Classification of mammals

To understand plants and animals, scientists look at their similarities and differences and sort them into groups. This is called classification.

Grouping plants and animals

Plants are divided into flowering plants and non-flowering plants. Animals are divided into those with backbones (vertebrates) and those without backbones (invertebrates).

Grouping vertebrates

Vertebrates are divided into five main groups (called classes). These classes include mammals.

Vertebrates

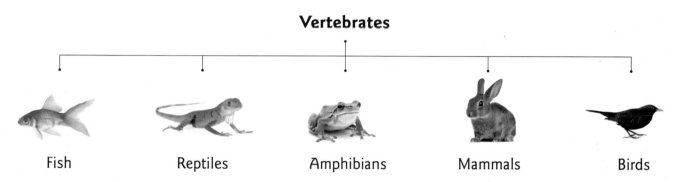

Fish   Reptiles   Amphibians   Mammals   Birds

From order to species

Mammals with similar features are divided into around 29 smaller groups called orders. These include primates, carnivores, rodents and bats.

Mammals

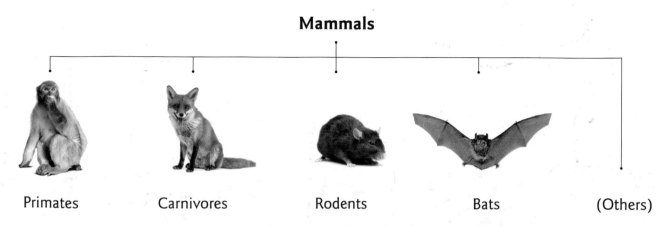

Primates   Carnivores   Rodents   Bats   (Others)

Orders are further divided into families and then genera. Species are the smallest groups – they are types of mammals that are so similar that they can breed together.

Glossary

adapted changed to suit the environment

bat box a box designed as a roosting place for bats

birds of prey birds that feed on animal flesh

breeding season the time of year when animals mate and produce young

burrows tunnels dug in the ground by animals

canines large teeth near the front of an animal's mouth

coniferous of trees that reproduce by making cones

conservation protecting and preserving natural environments and animals

cubs young animals, such as those of a fox

domesticated used to describe an animal that has been tamed and is used to living with people

extinct of a species of animal that has no living members

grazers animals that feed on grass and other low-growing plants

habitat a place where animals or plants live

hibernate to spend the winter in a deep sleep

incisor a tooth with a cutting edge

moors areas of rough land covered with low-growing plants

order a rank of living things made up of families that share similar characteristics

predators animals that hunt other animals

rodents mammals with sharp incisor teeth used for gnawing

roosting settling to rest or sleep

rump the back part of an animal

scavenging feeding on dead or decaying animals and waste

species a type of animal or plant that breeds with others of the same kind

territory an area of land that is lived in by an animal

warm-blooded of animals that keep a constant body temperature

Index